Mantras And Shlokas For Kids

Illustrated daily guide

By Sujata Saha

This book belongs to:

....

For permission
Contact: info.divinebharat@gmail.com
ISBN: 978-93-342-4868-5 Paperback

Find us at
https://www.divinebharat.co

Contents

Introduction

Chanting mantras has been an integral part of Indian tradition. From the moment we wake up in the morning to when we go to sleep, specific mantras are chanted to bring positivity, focus, and divine blessings into our lives. Whether before bathing, eating, studying, beginning a new task, or during puja, these sacred chants help set the right intention and bring peace to the mind.

Mantras were formulated by sages thousands of years ago. Their rhythmic sounds create a sense of calm, enhance concentration, and instil a sense of gratitude. Teaching children these mantras helps them grow into compassionate, mindful, and confident individuals. When a child chant a mantra, they connect with their inner self and experience the joy of spiritual harmony.

This book introduces children to these beautiful and meaningful mantras simply and engagingly. Each mantra is in Hindi and English, along with an easy-to-understand explanation. The vibrant illustrations make learning fun and help children connect with the deeper meaning of each chant.

May this book be a gentle companion in your child's journey toward wisdom, peace, and spiritual growth. Let the sacred sounds of these mantras bring joy and positivity to their everyday life!

कराग्रे वसते लक्ष्मीः करमध्ये सरस्वती ।
करमूले तु गोविन्दः प्रभाते करदर्शनम ॥

Morning Mantra

karagre vasate lakshmi karamadhye sarasvati |
karamule tu govinda prabhate kara darshanam ||

Meaning

At the Top of the Palm dwell Devi Lakshmi, at the Middle of the Palm dwell Devi Saraswati,
At the Bottom of the Palm dwell Sri Govinda; Therefore one should Look at one's Palms in early morning.

ॐ भूर् भुवः स्वः। तत् सवितुर्वरेण्यं।
भर्गो देवस्य धीमहि। धियो यो नः प्रचोदयात् ॥

Gayatri Mantra

Om Bhur Bhuvah Swaha Tat Savitur Varenyam |
Bhargo Devasya Dhimahi Dhiyo Yo Nah Pracho Dayat ||

Meaning

We meditate on that most adored Supreme Lord, the creator, whose effulgence (divine light) illumines all realms (physical, mental and spiritual). May this divine light illumine our intellect.

समुद्रवसने देवि पर्वतस्तनमंडले ।
विष्णुपत्नि नमस्तुभ्यं पादस्पर्श क्षमस्व मे ॥

Bhoomi Mantra

Samudra-Vasane Devi Parvata-Stana-Mandale |
Vishnu-Patni Namas-Tubhyam Paada-Sparsham Kssamasva-Me ||

Meaning

Oh Mother Earth,
You Who have the Ocean as Your Garments,
and Mountains as Your Bosom,
O Consort of Lord Vishnu, Salutations to You;
Please Forgive as my feet touch your Holy Body.

गङ्गे च यमुने चैव गोदावरि सरस्वति ।
नर्मदे सिन्धु कावेरि जलेऽस्मिन् संनिधिं कुरु ॥

Ritualistic Bath Mantra

Gange Cha Yamune Chaiva
Godavari Saraswathi |
Narmade Sindhu Kaveri
Jalesmin Sannidhim Kuru ||

Meaning

O Ganges, Yamuna, Godavari, Sarasvatī, Narmada, Sindhu and Kaveri, please make your presence felt in this water.

वक्रतुण्ड महाकाय सूर्यकोटि समप्रभ ।
निर्विघ्नं कुरु मे देव सर्वकार्येषु सर्वदा ॥

Obstacle Removal Mantra

Vakra-Tunndda Maha-Kaaya
Suurya-Kotti Samaprabha |
Nirvighnam Kuru Me Deva
Sarva-Kaaryessu Sarvadaa ||

Meaning

Salutations to the one Who has a Curved Trunk,
Large Body and Whose Splendour is
similar to Million Suns,
O God, Please remove all Obstacles in All my Works
Always by extending Your Blessings

शुभं करोति कल्याणमरोग्यं धनसंपदा।
शत्रुबुद्धिविनाशय दीपज्योतिर्नमोऽस्तुते ॥

Deepjyoti Mantra

Shubham karoti kalyaanam
Aarogyam dhana sampadaa I
Shatrubudhi vinaashaaya
Deepajyoti namoastute II

Meaning

The one who is our light, which brings auspiciousness, prosperity, sound health, abundant wealth, and destroys the intellect's enemy, our salutations to you

कर्पूरगौरं करुणावतारं संसारसारम् भुजगेन्द्रहारम् ।
सदावसन्तं हृदयारविन्दे भवं भवानीसहितं नमामि ॥

Shiva Mantra

Karpua Gauram Karunavataram

Sansarsaram Bhujagendraharam |

Sadavasantam Hridayaravinde

Bhavam Bhavanisahitam Namami ||

Meaning

The divine one, who is pure as camphor, who is an embodiment of compassion, the true spirit of the universe, one who draped the serpent king, one who resides in the heart that is pure as lotus. I bow to Lord Shiva and his consort Goddess Bhavani

ॐ त्र्यम्बकं यजामहे सुगन्धिं पुष्टिवर्धनम् ।
उर्वारुकमिव बन्धनान् मृत्योर्मुक्षीय मामृतात् ॥

Protection mantra

Om Try Ambakam Yajaamahe

Sugandhim Pushtti Vardhanam

Urvaarukamiva Bandhanaan

Mrityor Mukshiiya Maamrtaat ||

Meaning

Om, We Worship the Three-Eyed One,

Who is Fragrant, Increasing our Nourishment.

So that we are freed from the Bondages of Samsara

and Liberated from Death to Immortality.

Food Blessing Mantra

ओ३म् अन्नपतेऽन्नस्य नो देह्यनमीवस्य शुष्मिणः ।
प्र प्रदातारं तारिष ऊर्ज्जं नो धेहि द्विपदे चतुष्पदे ॥
ओ३म् शान्तिः शान्तिः शान्तिः ॥

Om Annapate annasya
no dehyana-meevasya shushminah,
Pra pradaataaram taarish oorjam
no dhehi dvipade chatushpade.
Om Shantih, Shantih, Shantih

Meaning

O Lord, Provider of a variety of food
Thank you for giving us food today.
May this food be decease-free,
nourishing, and good for my body, mind and soul.
May all people, animals and all creatures
receive their sustenance every day.
Let there be Peace.

सरस्वति नमस्तुभ्यं वरदे कामरूपिणि ।
विद्यारम्भं करिष्यामि सिद्धिर्भवतु मे सदा ॥

Saraswati Mantra

sarasvati namastubhyam varade kamarupini I
vidyarambha karisyami siddhirbhavatu me sada II

Meaning

Salutation to you, O Saraswathi, grantor of blessings and the one who fulfill of wishes. May there be success for me forever as I am starting my studies.

Student–Teacher Harmony Mantra

ॐ सह नाववतु ।

सह नौ भुनक्तु ।

सह वीर्यं करवावहै ।

तेजस्वि नावधीतमस्तु मा विद्विषावहै ।

ॐ शांतिः शांतिः शांतिः ॥

Om Saha Nau-Avatu |

Saha Nau Bhunaktu |

Saha Viiryam Karavaavahai |

Tejasvi Nau-Adhiitam-Astu Maa Vidvissaavahai |

Om Shaantih Shaantih Shaantih ||

Meaning

May we be protected.

May we be nourished together.

May we work vigorously together.

And may our studies illuminate us.

May there will be no conflict between us.

Let there be peace peace peace.

Guru Vandana

गुरूर्ब्रह्मा गुरूर्विष्णुः गुरूर्देवो महेश्वरः ।
गुरूर्साक्षात परब्रह्म तस्मै श्री गुरवे नमः ।।
ध्यानमूलं गुरोर्मूर्तिः पूजामूलं गुरोः पदम् ।
मंत्रमूलं गुरोर्वाक्यं मोक्षमूलं गुरोः कृपा ।।
अखण्डमण्डलाकारं व्याप्तं येन चराचरम् ।
तत्पदं दर्शितं येन तस्मै श्रीगुरवे नमः ।।

Gurur Brahma Gurur Vishnuh Gurur Devo Maheshvarah I

Gurur Sakshat Parabrahma Tasmai Shri Gurave Namah II

Dhyanamulam Gurormurtih Pujamulam Guroh Padam I

Mantramulam Guror Vakyam Mokshamulam Guroh Kripa II

Akhandamandalakaram Vyaptam Yena Characharam I

Tatpadam Darshitam Yena Tasmai Shri Gurave Namah II

Meaning

Guru is Brahma (creator), Vishnu (sustainer), and Shiva (destroyer). Guru is the Supreme Absolute. Salutations to the Guru. Meditation begins with the Guru's form, worship with the Guru's feet, mantra with the Guru's words, and liberation with the Guru's grace.Salutations to the Guru, who reveals the ultimate truth and pervades the entire universe.

ॐ असतो मा सद्गमय ।
तमसो मा ज्योतिर्गमय ।
मृत्योर्मा अमृतं गमय ।
ॐ शांतिः शांतिः शांतिः ॥

Peace Invocation

Om Asato Maa Sad-Gamaya |

Tamaso Maa Jyotir-Gamaya |

Mrityor-Maa Amrtam Gamaya |

Om Shaantih Shaantih Shaantih ||

Meaning

Om, (O Lord) Lead me

from the world of Unreal towards the Reality,

from the Darkness towards the Light,

from Mortality towards Immortality.

Om, Let there be Peace, Peace, Peace.

Divine Oneness Mantra

ॐ पूर्णमदः पूर्णमिदं पूर्णात्पूर्णमुदच्यते ।

पूर्णस्य पूर्णमादाय पूर्णमेवावशिष्यते ॥

ॐ शांतिः शांतिः शांतिः ॥

Om Poornnam-Adah Poornnam-Idam

Poornnaat-Poornnam-Udacyate |

Poornnasya Poornnam-Aadaaya

Poornnam-Eva-Avashissyate ||

Om Shaantih Shaantih Shaantih ||

Meaning

Om, The Outer World or Brahman is complete,

The individual self is also complete,

Taking away Purna from Purna, that means..

Although Individual is manifestation of Brahman,

infinite Brahma still remains.

Om, Peace, Peace, Peace.

यादेवी सर्वभूतेषु निद्रारूपेण संस्थिता ।
नमस्तस्यै नमस्तस्यै नमस्तस्यै नमोनमः ।

Sleep Mantra

Ya Devi Sarva Bhuteshu

Nidra Rupena Samsthita I

Namastasyai Namastasyai

Namastasyai Namo Namah II

Meaning

The Goddess expresses herself in the form of Sleep.

The Sleeping state in us is a form of the Mother Divine.

I bow to the Divine.

सर्वमङ्गलमाङ्गल्ये शिवे सर्वार्थसाधिके ।
शरण्ये त्र्यम्बके गौरि नारायणि नमोऽस्तु ते ॥

Durga Mantra

Sarva-Manggala-Maanggalye
Shive Sarvaartha-Saadhike |
Sharannye Tryambake Gauri
Naarayani Namohstute ||

Meaning

O Shive, Who is the Auspiciousness in All the Auspicious, Complete with All the Auspicious Attributes. Who fulfills All the Objectives of the Devotees .Who is the Giver of Refuge, Three Eyed Gauri, Salutations to You O Narayani.

Vishnu Mantra

शान्ताकारं भुजगशयनं पद्मनाभं सुरेशं
विश्वाधारं गगनसदृशं मेघवर्णं शुभाङ्गम् ।
लक्ष्मीकान्तं कमलनयनं योगिभिर्ध्यानगम्यं
वन्दे विष्णुं भवभयहरं सर्वलोकैकनाथम् ॥

Shaantakaaram Bhujaga-Shayanam
Padma-Naabham Suresham
Vishvadhaaram Gagana-Sadrsham
Megha-Varnnam Shubha-Anggam |
Lakssmii-Kaantam Kamala-Nayanam
Yogibhir-Dhyaana-Gamyam
Vande Vissnnum Bhava-Bhaya-Haram
Sarva-Lokaika-Naatham ||

Meaning

One Who Has a Serene Appearance. Who is Lying on the Bed of Serpent. From Whose Navel is springing up a Lotus and One who is presiding over the various elements of the Creations. Who is Boundless and Infinite like the Sky, Whose Bluish Colour is like the Cloud, which is radiating Auspiciousness. Who is the Beloved of Devi Lakshmi and has Lotus petals like Beautiful Eyes, Who is Attainable only through Meditation by the Yogis. I Worship that All-Pervading Vishnu Who Removes the Wordly Fear and Who is the Lord of All the Worlds.

नमस्तेस्तू महामाये श्रीपिठे सूरपुजिते ।
शंख चक्र गदा हस्ते महालक्ष्मी नमोस्तूते ॥

Mahalaxmi Mantra

Namastestu Mahamaye Shree Pithe Sura Poojite
Shanka Chakra Gadha Haste Maha Lakshmi
Namoostute |

Meaning

I bow to you O Mahamaya, the one who resides in Sripetha and is worshipped by devas,
The one who holds a conch, disc, and mace in her hands, I bow to the Goddess Mahalakshmi.

कृष्णाय वासुदेवाय हरये परमात्मने ।

प्रणतः क्लेशनाशाय गोविंदाय नमो नमः ।।

Krishna Mantra

krisnaya vasudevaya haraye paramatmane |
pranatah klesanasaya govindaya namo namah ||

Meaning

Salutation to Krishna, Vaasudeva, Hari the Paramatman, Govinda, we bow our heads to you for the destruction of all our grief.

राम रामेति रामेति, रमे रामे मनोरमे ।
सहस्रनाम तत्तुल्यं, रामनाम वरानने ॥

Rama Mantra

Ram Raameti Raameti, Rame Raame Manorame I
Sahasra-Nama Tat-Tulyam, Raama-Naama Varanane

Meaning

Rama means the name of Sita's husband. Rama is beautiful. Reciting Rama's name is pleasant to heart. Reciting This Rama name is equal to reciting Vishnu's thousand names.

ॐ सर्वे भवन्तु सुखिनः सर्वे सन्तु निरामयाः।
सर्वे भद्रान्नि पश्यन्तु माँ कश्चिद्-दुःख-भाग-भवेत्।
ॐ शांतिः शांतिः शांतिः॥

Universal peace Mantra

Om Sarve Bhavantu Sukhinah

Sarve Santu Niraamayaah |

Sarve Bhadraanni Pashyantu

Maa Kashcid-Duhkha-Bhaag-Bhavet |

Om Shaantih Shaantih Shaantih ||

Meaning

Om, May All be Happy,

May All be Free from Illness.

May All See what is Auspicious,

May no one Suffer.

Om Peace, Peace, Peace.

www.ingramcontent.com/pod-product-compliance
Lightning Source LLC
Chambersburg PA
CBHW061316170726
48282CB00020B/110
* 9 7 8 9 3 3 4 2 4 8 6 8 5 *